THE RAILROAD

IN AMERICAN HISTORY

THE BIRTH OF THE LOCOMOTIVE
(1780s–1820s)

Joanne Mattern

Mitchell Lane
PUBLISHERS

P.O. Box 196
Hockessin, Delaware 19707

THE RAILROAD

IN AMERICAN HISTORY

The Birth of the Locomotive
The Railroad Comes to America
The Railroad Grows into an Industry
The Railroad and the Civil War
The Railroad Fuels Westward Expansion
Electric Trains and Trolleys

The publisher would like to thank Milton C. Hallberg for acting as a consultant on its *The Railroad in American History* series. He is a professor emeritus of agricultural economics at Pennsylvania State University and has been a visiting professor at universities around the world. His railroad interests began when he attended a railroad telegraphers' school in preparation for a job as a depot agent on the CB&Q Railroad in Illinois. After retiring from teaching, he returned to his railroad interests as a new hobby, during which time he has written about early rail systems.

PUBLISHER'S NOTE:

The facts on which this book is based have been thoroughly researched. Documentation of such research can be found on page 44. While every possible effort has been made to ensure accuracy, the publisher will not assume liability for damages caused by inaccuracies in the data, and makes no warranty on the accuracy of the information contained herein.

Printing
1   2   3   4   5   6   7   8   9

**Library of Congress
Cataloging-in-Publication Data**
Mattern, Joanne, 1963-
 The birth of the locomotive (1780–1820) / by Joanne Mattern.
     p. cm. —(The railroad in American history)
 Includes bibliographical references and index.
 ISBN 978-1-61228-286-2 (library bound)
 1. Locomotives—History--Juvenile literature. 2. Railroads—History--Juvenile literature. I. Title.
 TJ605.5.M38 2013
 385.3'6—dc23
                                    2012009415

eBook ISBN: 9781612283609

PLB

CONTENTS

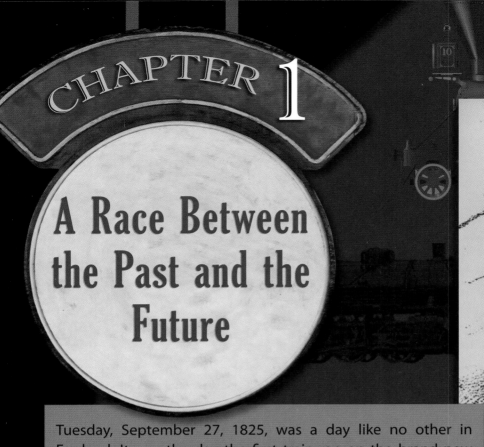

CHAPTER 1

A Race Between the Past and the Future

Tuesday, September 27, 1825, was a day like no other in England. It was the day the first train ran on the brand new Stockton and Darlington Railway. Thousands of people gathered to see this amazing invention that would change the world. They came on horseback, in wagons, and on foot. Many believed the "absurd scheme" would fail, according to an early account.[1]

The freshly painted locomotive, which later became known as *Locomotion,* was waiting on the tracks, a short distance from the Masons Arms pub in Shildon. Behind the locomotive sat its tender, carrying water and coal to power the engine. Twelve wagons loaded with coal and one carrying sacks of flour rolled up were attached to the locomotive. Excited riders perched on top of the loads.

Another twenty-one wagons were also attached. They were crammed with passengers—railroad workers, engineers, and even members of the public who had been invited by the railroad to take a free ride that day. Only 300 were

Opening of the Stockton and Darlington Railway in 1825.

The Experiment was specially built to carry passengers on the Stockton and Darlington Railway's opening day. The coach carried eighteen passengers on what must have been a bumpy and uncomfortable ride. Later, the coach was pulled along the railway by horses, as only freight was hauled by locomotives.

supposed to ride, but more than 500 excited people had jostled and pushed their way aboard.[2]

Still another wagon was hooked on. This special carriage, called *The Experiment,* carried the people who had invested their money in the new railroad. It had room for eighteen people sitting on long, padded benches that faced each other.

George Stephenson, who had designed the locomotive, was given the honor of driving *Locomotion.* Finally, with a blast of steam that caused many of the people standing near the tracks to scatter in fear, the engine moved out with its eighty-ton load. A man on a horse rode in front of the train.

A bystander described the scene: "The excitement was intense. On went the pilot, after him the train. All along the road and embankment were crowds—rushing, running, riding, cheering, galloping along, in sight of the train till Stephenson, telling the horse pilot to get out of the road, put on steam and soon left the excited multitudes panting in the rear."[3]

The nine-mile journey from Shildon to the market town of Darlington took two hours. That included three stops, one of them to remove a broken wagon from the train. As the train chugged into Darlington, almost all of the town's residents turned out to watch. The train stopped and some of the coal was distributed for free to the poor people of the town. A brass band climbed into the empty coal wagons to play music for the rest of the historic journey to Stockton. Still more riders climbed aboard, too, clinging to the wagons "like a swarm of bees," according to author Michael Heavisides.[4]

People came from miles around to see the new Stockton and Darlington Railway. For many, it was the first time they had seen a locomotive.

A stagecoach

For part of the trip, the railway ran alongside a public road. One of the most exciting moments on the journey occurred when the train came upon a stagecoach with four horses pulling sixteen passengers. For a while, the stagecoach and the train traveled neck and neck in what Heavisides called a race between "the past and the future."[5] It didn't take long before the horses fell back and the locomotive surged ahead, reaching speeds of fifteen miles (twenty-four kilometers) per hour.

The train, filled with cheering passengers, finally pulled into Stockton at 3:45 in the afternoon. As the train steamed into the station, a twenty-one-gun salute boomed and a huge, waiting crowd yelled with excitement. The passengers celebrated late into the evening, toasting the day's historic journey.

The Stockton and Darlington Railway was the first commercial railway in the world. It had taken many years of work, failure, and innovation to get to that day. The birth of the locomotive meant amazing changes for England and later, the United States and the world.

"Father of the Railways"

George
Stephenson

George Stephenson was one of the most important locomotive engineers and eventually became known as the "Father of the Railways." He was born on June 9, 1781, in the village of Wylam in northeastern England. Wylam was near Newcastle, one of the main producers of coal in Great Britain. Stephenson came from a mining family and his house was next to a path where wagons traveled back and forth between the colliery (the mine and its buildings) and the Tyne River, from where it was shipped all over England. Stephenson worked at several mines as a young man. He was fascinated by machines and often took apart the engines in the colliery to see how they worked. The owners of one mine noticed his talent and soon put Stephenson in charge of repairing and maintaining all of the engines in the mine.

Stephenson went on to invent and build a variety of steam-powered engines. He also invented a new type of safety lamp that would not explode when it was exposed to flammable gases in the mines. Later he became the chief engineer for several major railway lines. Stephenson's work made him rich and famous, and earned him a place in history as the "Father of the Railways." He married three times and was survived by his only son, Robert, who also became a famous railway engineer. George Stephenson died at his home, Tapton House, on August 12, 1848, at the age of sixty-seven.

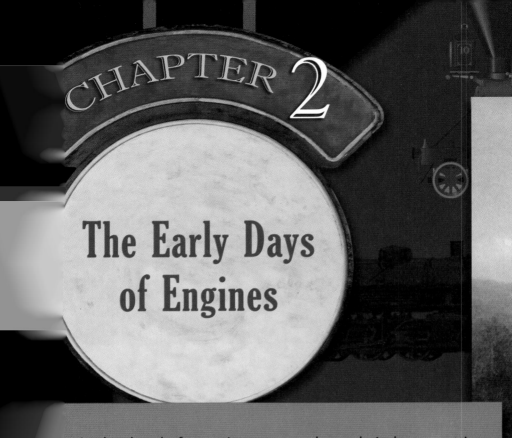

CHAPTER 2

The Early Days of Engines

In the days before trains, cars, trucks, and airplanes, getting goods from one place to another was a big problem all over the world. In the newly formed United States, people who lived along the coast had to rely on ships to bring food and supplies to their cities and towns. People who lived inland depended on canals and rivers for passageways.

Horse-drawn wagons were also used to carry freight around the young nation. A large covered wagon such as the Conestoga wagon could carry up to eight tons of freight with a team of six horses or oxen doing the pulling. These wagons could even float like barges when they crossed rivers.

People also needed to travel from one place to another. They could walk, ride horses, or travel by horse-drawn coaches or carriages. If they were lucky enough to live near the coast or an inland waterway, they could travel by ship.

A Conestoga wagon

All of these methods of travel had one thing in common. They were slow. A barge might average only five miles (eight kilometers) an hour. At this rate of speed, it took days or weeks for goods to reach an inland city from the coast. This was much too long for perishable goods such as vegetables, fruit, fish, and meat. These items would spoil before they could reach their destination. Horse-drawn travel was also difficult and often dangerous. Wagons had to travel over rutted dirt paths that could become a sea of mud after a rainstorm.

People needed a better, faster way to travel and move goods from one place to another. The answer to this problem was the railroad. However, the railroad did not develop overnight. It took many baby steps before trains were rolling all over Europe and the United States.

The idea for railroads began in Europe hundreds of years ago. As far back as the 1550s, miners in Germany were moving heavy loads of ore by shoveling it onto carts and then running the carts along smooth

Since mines are deep underground, it is very difficult to haul cargo up to the surface. This photo shows an old German mine cart, which would have carried the mine's contents on steep, narrow passageways.

tracks instead of dragging them over uneven ground. The miners set parallel tracks of wooden planks on the ground. The carts had a pin that rode in the groove between the planks to keep them from running off the tracks. Soon, this type of "wagonway" was being used in other parts of Europe, including England.

By the early 1700s, English mining companies were using a system of parallel wooden rails that let horses pull heavily loaded carts between mines and canals. The rails were attached to wooden crossties that kept them an equal distance apart. By the mid-1700s, they were using strap-iron rails, made with thin strips of cast iron fixed onto wooden rails. By the early 1800s, they were using cast-iron rails and iron wheels. Horses still did all the pulling along these tramways, which allowed the miners to move heavier loads much more quickly. However, this system was not powerful enough to move large loads of freight over long distances. These things would not be possible until inventors harnessed the power of steam.

Thomas Savery got a patent for the first crude steam engine in 1698. The first commercially successful steam engine was built by Thomas Newcomen and used as early as 1712 in England. It pumped water out of flooded coal mines, so people could dig farther.

Newcomen's engine was very basic and it was very big. It used air pressure to work, so it was called an atmospheric engine. Water was heated inside a tank, called a boiler, by a coal fire underneath. The hot water turned into steam. A valve at the top of the boiler could be opened to let the steam flow into a cylinder.

The cylinder contained a piston that was able to move up and down. As the piston rose to the top of the cylinder, steam was let in underneath it. Then the steam valve was closed and a second valve was snapped open briefly. This valve let a spray of cold water into the cylinder. The cold water hit the steam and made it condense, or shrink, which created a vacuum. The vacuum was weaker than the pressure of the air outside the cylinder, which was open at the top. The air pressure pushed the piston down.

Newcomen's engine was originally used to pump water out of the mines. It was the first practical steam engine, but it was not powerful or efficient enough to be used for transportation.

A rod on the piston was attached to a chain that led straight up to one end of a huge beam atop a strong wall. The beam could rock in the same way as a playground seesaw. When air pushed the piston down in the cylinder, the attached chain pulled down that side of the beam. The beam's other side rose. It was attached to a rod that powered the pump deep within the mine.

The pump side of the beam was heavier than the piston side. Once it rocked as high as it could go, gravity made that side of the beam sink back down. As it sank, the side of the beam attached to the piston rod rose and pulled the piston back to the top of the cylinder. As the piston rose, the steam valve was reopened. The cylinder filled with steam again, and the entire process was repeated.

On the very early engines, the valves were opened and closed by miners who stood by, waiting for the slow build-up of steam. The piston only moved up and down about twelve times a minute. Soon, people figured out how to make the engine itself open and close the valves.

The Industrial Revolution Begins

Newcomen's steam engine was not very efficient. The cylinder had to be heated and cooled for each up-and-down stroke of the piston. Lots of coal had to be burned for this process. During the 1760s, a Scottish engineer named James Watt was asked to repair a Newcomen engine. Watt saw that heating and cooling the cylinder over and over was a big waste of energy and steam. For the next twenty years, he worked on improving Newcomen's engine.

Watt noticed that boiler rooms were always very hot. One of his changes was to wrap the boiler with insulation to keep in the heat.

Watt also figured out that when a separate chamber containing a vacuum was connected to the cylinder, the steam would rush into that chamber where it could be condensed without cooling the cylinder. This separate condenser let the cylinder stay hot all the time, which saved energy. Watt closed the top of the cylinder and injected low-pressure steam above the piston as well as below it. He used the force of expanding steam instead of air pressure to move the piston up and down in his double-acting cylinder.

Most importantly, Watt came up with a way for his engine to supply rotary, or circular, motion. He attached the piston rod to a gear, which turned a second gear. The spinning second gear was attached to a flywheel and driveshaft. This spinning driveshaft could power all sorts of equipment, not just a pump.

By the 1790s, Watt had improved the steam engine so much that it began to change the world. Once machines could be run by steam, they could work harder and faster than humans. Steam engines were used in factories, mills, and other businesses. It wasn't long before several clever engineers saw that steam could also power an engine that would be strong enough to pull a train. Quite a few people tried to create this engine, but their first attempts did not work very well.

In 1769, a Frenchman named Nicolas Joseph Cugnot built a steam-powered carriage. The three-wheeled carriage was designed to move heavy weapons such as cannons across a battlefield. However, the

slow-moving carriage was a failure. Its engine ran out of steam quickly. The boiler had to be refilled with water and the flames in its small firebox relit after only about fifteen minutes. Then everyone had to wait until the steam built up before they could try moving it again. Another problem was the design. Cugnot had mounted the huge, heavy boiler over the single front wheel. This made the carriage unstable, which was a real problem since it was meant to travel on rugged battlefields. Cugnot's invention was abandoned.

James Watt also toyed with the idea of creating a steam-powered engine that could be used for transportation. In 1784, he took out a patent for a wheeled carriage that would be powered by a steam engine. However, Watt never actually built his carriage. He realized that he would need to use steam under very high pressure to make the carriage work. That idea made Watt nervous.

In 1784, another Englishman, William Murdoch, built a model of a steam-powered carriage. Murdoch's foot-high carriage used one cylinder and high-pressure steam. However, Watt still held the patent for a steam carriage. He warned Murdoch to stop his work or face legal action.

Six years later, in 1790, a Colonial American named Nathan Read applied for a patent for a steam carriage that would have two cylinders, one for each front wheel. His design had another important feature. Read knew that for steam engines to be practical in vehicles, a smaller boiler was needed. He came up with the idea of building a boiler that had the fire inside of it instead of underneath. He also put many water tubes inside the boiler. This system was called multi-tubular. Later multi-tubular systems would put the heat inside the tubes and pass them through the water in the boiler.

It would be a few more years before another Englishman would come up with a steam engine that would lead to the birth of the locomotive.

A Dangerous Thing

Old Bess, the oldest surviving Watt beam engine, used low-pressure steam.

James Watt was terrified of using steam under high pressure. He had good reason. Steam is created when water boils and turns into a vapor. That vapor is extremely hot—more than 212 degrees Fahrenheit (100 degrees Celsius), the boiling point of water. Steam under high pressure can make its container explode. An explosion of high-pressure steam would cause severe burns or even death to anyone unlucky enough to be nearby. It would also blow apart the engine, sending metal pieces whizzing through the air at high speed.

The good thing about high-pressure steam is that it produces a lot of energy. Watt's engines always worked at pressures below ten pounds per square inch (10 psi). However, this low pressure did not provide a lot of power. If Watt had been brave enough to put his steam under higher pressure, he would have created more energy in an engine that could have accomplished bigger tasks. Watt's fear kept him from designing a working steam locomotive. Because a locomotive has to be able to provide a constant source of high energy, Watt's methods would never allow him to build an engine that would work for transporting heavy loads or large numbers of passengers.

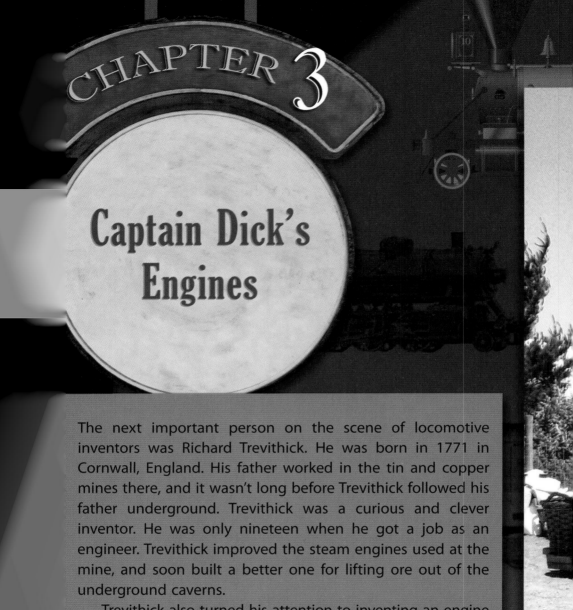

CHAPTER 3

Captain Dick's Engines

The next important person on the scene of locomotive inventors was Richard Trevithick. He was born in 1771 in Cornwall, England. His father worked in the tin and copper mines there, and it wasn't long before Trevithick followed his father underground. Trevithick was a curious and clever inventor. He was only nineteen when he got a job as an engineer. Trevithick improved the steam engines used at the mine, and soon built a better one for lifting ore out of the underground caverns.

Trevithick also turned his attention to inventing an engine that could be used for transportation. He knew it would need to use high-pressure steam to be small enough and strong enough to move a vehicle. In 1796, he began building models of engines that could move a vehicle. He had seen the model steam carriage built by his neighbor William Murdoch. Trevithick was one of the first inventors to use miniatures, a practice that is still standard procedure today.

A replica of the *Puffing Devil*

Trevithick built his models at home, and his wife often talked about how they puffed around the house. In a book he wrote about his father, Francis Trevithick described a time when visitors came to see one model. "Lord and Lady Dedunstanville, the large landed Proprietors in the mining district . . . and Mr. Davies Gilbert, a friend of Trevithick's, came to her house to see the model work. A boiler, something like a strong iron kettle, was placed on the fire; Davies Gilbert was stoker, and blew the bellows; Lady Dedunstanville was engine man, and turned the cock for the admission of steam to the first high-pressure steam-engine. The model was made of bright brass."[1]

Trevithick spent several years perfecting his models. Then he used what he had learned to build a full-size engine. On December 24, 1801, he was ready to show off his invention. He invited several of his friends to ride on his road locomotive. His high-pressure steam engine eliminated Watt's condenser by venting exhaust steam through a pipe and into the air. He called the engine *Puffing Devil* because of the noise it made as the steam was released. Trevithick's friends nicknamed the engine "Captain Dick's Puffer."

Puffing Devil was not meant to travel on rails. Instead it traveled on the road. The engine had one double-acting cylinder—meaning steam pushed on both sides of the piston to move it up and down. The piston was attached to a crank that turned a large flywheel. As the piston moved up and down, the crank turned the flywheel. The flywheel was attached to the locomotive's wheels, so when it turned, it moved the locomotive's wheels.

Trevithick and his friends climbed aboard *Puffing Devil* and started off. The trip went well at first, even though it was raining hard and the road was rough and slippery. One of the passengers, Stephen Williams, later told Francis Trevithick about the adventure, and Francis included the story in his biography of his father. "In the year 1801, upon Christmas-eve, coming on evening, Captain Dick got up steam, out in the high-road, just outside the shop at the Weith. When we see'd that Captain Dick was agoing to turn on steam, we jumped up as many as

The *Puffing Devil* was an exciting development in locomotive technology, but it could only travel short distances before it ran out of steam. A replica, or copy, of the locomotive can still be seen today and is sometimes taken out on the road for special occasions.

could; may be seven or eight of us. 'Twas a stiffish hill going from the Weith up to Camborne Beacon, but she went off like a little bird. When she had gone about a quarter of a mile, there was a roughish piece of road covered with loose stones; she didn't go quite so fast, and as it was a flood of rain, and we were very squeezed together, I jumped off. She was going faster than I could walk, and went on up the hill about a quarter or half a mile farther, when they turned her and came back again to the shop. Captain Dick tried her again the next day I was not there, but heard say that some of the castings broke. Recollect seeing pieces of the engine in the ditch years afterwards, and suppose she ran against the hedge."[2]

Running on Rails

Richard Trevithick was not finished making locomotive engines. In 1803, Samuel Homfray, the owner of the Penydarren Ironworks in Wales, asked Trevithick to build a steam-powered vehicle. Homfray needed a locomotive that could haul iron from his factory to a canal nine miles (fourteen and a half kilometers) away. Unlike the *Puffing Devil,* this steam engine would need to run on rails.

Trevithick named his engine the *Penydarren,* after the factory. It was a large engine that weighed about five tons and featured a single cylinder, just like Trevithick's earlier engine, the *Puffing Devil.*

A test run of the *Penydarren* on February 13, 1804, was a success. The train ran a short distance along the tracks and back. In a letter to a friend two days later, Trevithick wrote that the engine "work'd very well,

The *Penydarren*

and ran uphill and downhill with great ease, and very manageable. We had plenty of steam and power."[3] It was the first recorded run by a railway locomotive.

In another letter to the same friend a week later, Trevithick noted, "The Tram Waggon have been at work several times. It works exceeding well, and is much more manageable than horses."[4] Trevithick also explained that the locomotive traveled 9 feet (2.7 meters) with every up-and-down stroke of the piston, which was a speed of just over 4 mph (6.5 km/h).

On February 21, the locomotive pulled a train of five wagons loaded with ten tons of iron and seventy passengers the full nine miles along the tracks. Everyone was excited, but that joy did not last. The *Penydarren* engine was very heavy, and the cast-iron rails could not support it. *Penydarren* only made a few trips before Homfray realized that his plan would not work. An engine that constantly broke the tracks was not an efficient way for him to transport his goods, so he stopped using the locomotive on the rails. Its wheels were removed, and it went into service as a stationary engine powering a forge hammer at the ironworks.

Trevithick kept on building locomotives. By 1808, he had built a locomotive he named *Catch Me Who Can*. It ran on a circular track and pulled a single carriage. People could buy a ticket and ride around and around at a speed of about twelve miles (nineteen kilometers) per hour. *Catch Me Who Can* was a popular attraction in the city of London for a short time. However, Trevithick faced the same problem that he had with Penydarren. His locomotive was so heavy it broke the tracks, and one time the locomotive tipped over. Soon after he opened the attraction, Trevithick closed it and abandoned *Catch Me Who Can* forever.

Trevithick never invented another locomotive, but he continued to improve the steam engines in use at that time. In 1812, he invented the Cornish boiler. Other boilers featured a coal-burning box underneath the tank that held the water. Trevithick changed this design. He put the

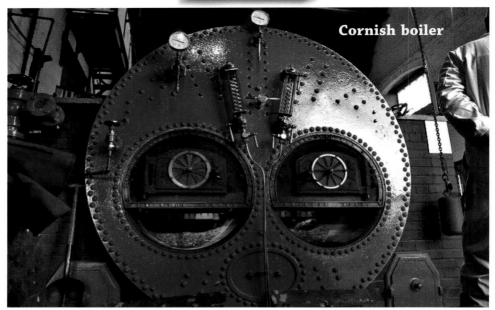

Cornish boiler

firebox inside the boiler. Heat from the firebox ran through a tube, or flue, in the middle of the water-filled boiler. This kept heat from escaping into the air before it passed through the boiler, and it allowed the coal to burn more efficiently. A Cornish boiler could do two or three times the work of other engines using the same amount of coal.

Although he was a brilliant inventor, Trevithick was a poor businessman. In 1811, he declared bankruptcy. A few years later, he left England to work in South America. Between 1816 and 1827, Trevithick supervised the installation of pumping engines in gold, silver, and copper mines in Peru and Colombia. He also worked in mines in the Central American nation of Costa Rica before returning to England in 1827. He was hired to develop an experimental engine for a steamship, and worked on the project until his death in 1833.

Many industrialists made a fortune off his work, but Trevithick was penniless when he died. His fellow workers took up a collection to pay for his funeral. He didn't seem to regret his choices, however. In a letter to his friend Davies Gilbert, he said "being a useful subject can never be taken from me, which to me far exceeds riches."[5]

Meanwhile, other engineers were working on their own engines, and Trevithick's work would inspire them to even better creations.

Making Rails Stronger

As Richard Trevithick soon found out, inventing a powerful locomotive was only part of the solution to creating a working railway. The other part was having rails strong enough to support the weight of the engine. During the early 1800s, rails were made of cast iron, which is very brittle and cracks easily. Cast iron rails were strong enough to support a wagon pulled by horses, but a locomotive weighing several tons was too much for them to handle. After only a few trips, the rails would crack and break. Inventors first tried to solve this problem by using a rail shaped like an upside-down letter T. This shape strengthened the rails, but not enough to keep the brittle iron from cracking.

Inventors needed to come up with a material that was stronger than iron. The answer was steel. Steel is made by mixing iron with other metals to make it stronger. Steel rails were a big step in the improvement of the railroad. Early rail systems in the United States suffered from the same problems, but by the time railroads were expanding to the west in the mid-1800s, almost all the rails were made of steel.

CHAPTER 4

A Blast of Steam

During the early 1800s, engineers continued to experiment with engines that could be used to power locomotives. They made improvements to other parts of the railway system, too.

In 1811, an engineer named John Blenkinsop patented a rail with metal teeth that stuck out and grabbed cogwheels on the locomotive. Since Blenkinsop worked at a mine where coal had to be carried three and a half miles (five and a half kilometers) on steep roads, his toothed cogwheels helped the locomotive stay on the tracks. In his rack-and-pinion system, the locomotive had four smooth wheels running along smooth tracks. These wheels held up the engine and rolled it along, but they weren't driving wheels— they didn't get power from the engine. The driving wheels were the toothed cogwheels, called pinions. Their teeth meshed with the toothed rail, called a rack rail. There was a rack rail on only one side of the track, but the locomotive

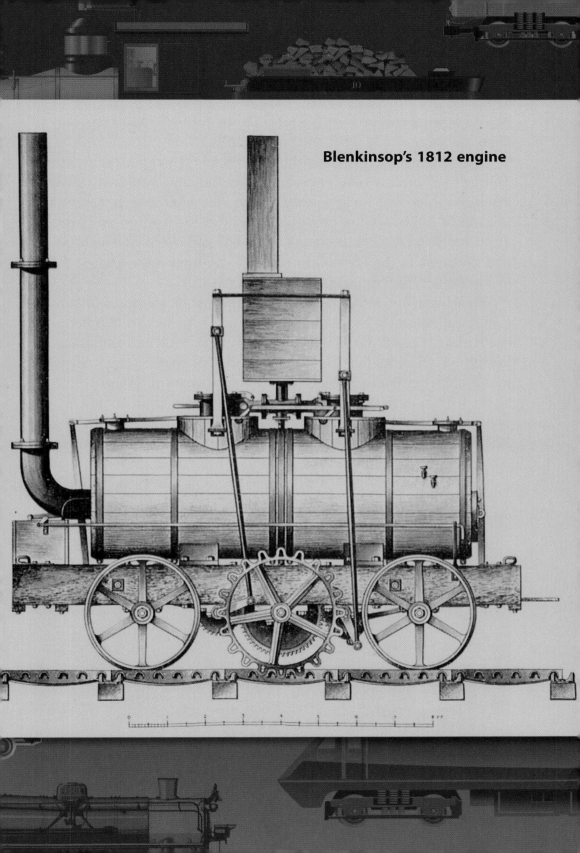

Blenkinsop's 1812 engine

had a cogwheel on each side, so it could be turned around regularly to even out wear and tear.[1]

While Blenkinsop designed the rails, his friend and partner, Matthew Murray, designed a new engine. Murray's engine had two cylinders instead of one. This arrangement meant that when one piston was at the top of its stroke, the other piston was at the bottom of its stroke. The pistons took turns pumping, so there was twice as much power and no break in the flow of power. The cylinders were located partly inside the top of the boiler to preserve heat.

Blenkinsop and Murray's system was the first railway to be financially successful. Murray's first engine ran from the colliery in Middleton to the harbor in Leeds, England, on June 24, 1812. It carried eight wagons loaded with twenty-five tons of coal and fifty people. The train went into regular operation, pulling up to thirty wagons at a time.

In 1813, an engineer named William Hedley built an engine for the Wylam colliery. Hedley called his engine *Puffing Billy*. The first *Puffing Billy* had four wheels, but it ran into a familiar problem. The heavy

Puffing Billy

engine broke the tracks. In 1815, Hedley changed to an eight-wheel design. Eight wheels distributed the weight of the engine more evenly and placed less stress on the rails.

Puffing Billy was a very reliable engine and was used for almost fifty years, until it was retired in 1862. Soon after he built *Puffing Billy,* Hedley built a similar engine named *Wylam Dilly,* which remained on the line until 1867. These engines worked at a steam pressure of 50 psi and could pull nine wagons at a speed of 4 to 5 mph (6.5 to 8 km/h). They were the first regular and reliable way to carry freight by a steam locomotive.

The next important engineer who would contribute to this field was another Englishman, George Stephenson. Stephenson went into the mines to work when he was fifteen years old. His first job was picking stones and other material from the coal before it was sent aboveground. Within a few years, he had been promoted and was in charge of operating and maintaining the engines in the mines.

Stephenson was fascinated with steam engines. In his spare time, he took them apart and put them back together. Stephenson did not have a lot of formal education—he didn't learn to read or write his own name until he was in his late teens—but he had a practical education that would help him become an engineer and inventor. He was also smart enough to know that he could learn a lot from the work of other inventors. When the first steam locomotives began running, he made a point of going to see them in action.

In 1813, Stephenson was watching one of Blenkinsop and Murray's steam engines pull a row of coal cars at a speed of about three miles (five kilometers) per hour. He was not very impressed and told a bystander that he could make a better engine. Stephenson set right to work on backing up his words. By 1814, he was ready to display his new invention.

Stephenson called his first steam locomotive the *Blücher.* It worked at the Killingworth colliery, and could pull eight cars carrying a total weight of thirty tons up a grade, or hill, at four miles (six kilometers)

per hour. Power was transferred from the engine to its four driving wheels by spur gears, or toothed cogwheels. After a year's trial, Stephenson figured out that it cost just as much to haul coal by steam power as by horses.

Almost as soon as he completed the first *Blücher*, Stephenson set about building a second engine that would be more economical. One

Unlike other locomotives, George Stephenson's *Blücher* had gears that drove the wheels directly. *Blücher* could pull 30 tons up a hill at 4 mph (6.4 km/h). Stephenson later said the *Blücher* was worth fifty horses in strength.

of the first things he did was remove the spur gears. Stephenson developed a system of rods to connect the pistons in the cylinders directly to the four driving wheels. Ball-and-socket joints were used where the rods attached to the crossheads of the piston rods and to the crankpins of the wheels. These joints let the engine bounce along uneven tracks without putting stress on its moving parts.

He also connected the two pairs of driving wheels so they rolled at the same speed. Stephenson wanted to use bars fastened to cranks in the axles, but workmen were not able to forge them. Instead, he used chains, which rolled over indented wheels at the center of each axle, the straight rod connecting each pair of wheels. In later locomotives, these cranks and bars were built and put into place on the outside of the wheels.

Stephenson also changed the design of the wheels. With other engines, the wheels often slipped off the tracks. This problem caused many accidents. Stephenson put a flange, or metal lip, on the inside edge of the wheels. This flange locked the wheels into place on the tracks.

The first *Blücher* had trouble generating enough steam to keep it running over a long distance. Stephenson found a solution to this problem by solving another problem. *Blücher* used a pipe to release exhaust steam from its cylinders into the air. As the steam released, it hissed loudly. Horses and cattle near the railroad were scared by the noise. One landowner was so angry he threatened to sue the Killingworth colliery. Stephenson was told to find a way to stop the terrible racket.

To stay out of trouble, Stephenson added a blast pipe to his engine. The blast pipe captured the exhaust steam and sent it into the engine's smokestack. There the steam mixed with the exhaust from the burning coals in the boiler, which created a vacuum. The vacuum made the fire burn hotter, which created more steam for the cylinders. This extra steam doubled the engine's power and helped the *Blücher* run faster and farther than any locomotive before it.

George Stephenson lived in this cottage on the grounds of the Killingworth colliery while he worked there as an engineer. He built his famous *Rocket* in the yard in back of the house.

For years, people argued about whether Stephenson had invented the blast pipe or copied one he had seen elsewhere. Some said he invented it only to make his engine quieter, not because he knew it would create so much power. Others said he was clever enough to realize that fast-escaping exhaust steam could help turn the engine's fire into a powerful blaze. One thing was certain: Steam-blast technology meant locomotives were getting much more powerful.

Another Father of the Railways

William Hedley

Although George Stephenson is usually called the "Father of the Railways," William Hedley can also lay claim to this title. Hedley was eight years younger than Stephenson and went to school in Stephenson's hometown of Wylam. Like Stephenson, Hedley was familiar with the Wylam tramway, a path that was traveled by horse-drawn wagons carrying coal from the mines. Also like Stephenson, Hedley got a job in a mine and had advanced to an important position by the time he was in his early twenties. In 1804, the owner of the Wylam colliery asked Hedley to build a locomotive. Hedley did, and was pleased when the engine ran successfully along the tracks at Wylam. However, the mine's owner did not use the engine, probably because it was too heavy for the rails.

Hedley went on to build other engines, several of which were closely studied by George Stephenson. Hedley tested his engines to answer a question that had been bothering engineers since Richard Trevithick designed his locomotive earlier in the century. The wheels on Trevithick's locomotive were smooth and ran on smooth rails, and he proved that this system would work without the wheels losing traction. However, engineers didn't think this concept would work if an engine carried a load that was heavier than the engine itself. Through his designs and tests, Hedley proved that an engine pulling a fully loaded train did indeed create enough friction to keep smooth wheels running on smooth rails, no matter how heavy the train was.

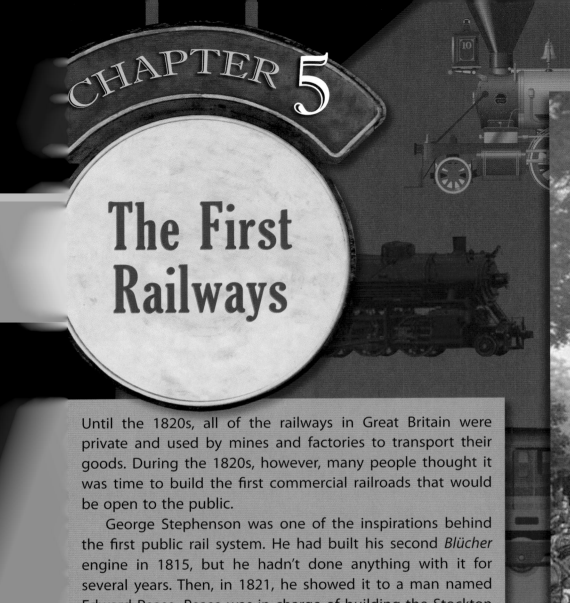

CHAPTER 5

The First Railways

Until the 1820s, all of the railways in Great Britain were private and used by mines and factories to transport their goods. During the 1820s, however, many people thought it was time to build the first commercial railroads that would be open to the public.

George Stephenson was one of the inspirations behind the first public rail system. He had built his second *Blücher* engine in 1815, but he hadn't done anything with it for several years. Then, in 1821, he showed it to a man named Edward Pease. Pease was in charge of building the Stockton and Darlington Railway in England. It would run from the Witton Park colliery to a town called Stockton, on the Tees River. The market town of Darlington was about halfway along the twenty-six-mile (forty-one-kilometer) route.

The railway got its start when Pease and his business partners obtained an act of Parliament in 1821. The act gave them legal permission to build a road for "the passage of wagons and other carriages from Stockton to Witton Park

Opening of the Stockton and Darlington Railway c1825 painted in the 1880s by John Dobbin.

Colliery, Darlington."[1] The line was originally designed as a public road that could be used by people riding in carriages and by freight wagons drawn by horses.

George Stephenson heard about Pease's plans and decided to convince Pease that a steam-powered railway would be a much better idea than a system using horses. Stephenson met with Pease in April of 1821 and astonished him with his idea of a steam-powered locomotive. At first, Pease didn't think this was a good idea. After all, horses were a tried-and-true form of transportation and everyone knew they would work. A locomotive pulling a train sounded like a ridiculous idea.

Stephenson did not give up. He met with Pease again and demonstrated his engine, the *Blücher*. Pease was so impressed by Stephenson's creation that he changed his mind. He went back to Parliament and got permission for locomotives to be used on the new railway, and he hired Stephenson to be its chief engineer. Stephenson was thrilled and immediately wrote to Pease, "I am glad to learn that the Parliament Bill has been passed for the Darlington Railway. I am much obliged by the favourable sentiments you express towards me, and shall be happy if I can be of service in carrying into execution your plans."[2]

It took four years to build the new railway. Finally, on September 27, 1825, a train ran along the tracks for the first time. The day was filled with celebration and triumph, although there was one tragedy. A man named John Stevens had grabbed onto a wagon to ride the train. He lost his grip and fell along the rails. The train ran over his foot, crushing it. A local newspaper reported that "medical men" said amputating his foot would be the only way to save his life, but there is no record of what happened to Stevens after that.[3]

The Stockton and Darlington Railway was a tremendous success. It remained in use for many years, carrying both freight and passengers. New towns sprang up along the train's route, as the area became more developed and easier to get around. Stephenson designed some of the first locomotives used on the line.

The *Royal George* was built by Timothy Hackworth. It had six wheels, unlike earlier locomotives, which ran on four wheels. Pistons and connecting rods powered the rear wheels.

Stephenson was very proud of his locomotives and was known to boast that he could see no way in which his engines might be improved. However, these early steam engines were unreliable and often broke down. In 1825, another engineer named Timothy Hackworth became the locomotive superintendent for the Stockton and Darlington Railway. He was determined to build a new engine. The result was the *Royal George.*

The boiler on the *Royal George* was 13 feet (4 meters) long and 4 feet 4 inches (1.3 meters) wide. Instead of a single flue running through the water in the boiler, this engine had a double flue. It greatly increased the heat of the water in the boiler. The engine had two vertical cylinders that connected to the rear axle. The other two axles on the six-wheeled locomotive were connected to the rear axle by metal beams. A blast pipe sent exhaust steam from the cylinders into the smokestack to create more power. In 1829, George Stephenson's son, Robert, who was also a talented engineer, called *Royal George* the most powerful locomotive that had yet been made.

During the 1820s, plans for an even bigger railway than the Stockton and Darlington were in the works. This railway would link the industrial cities of Liverpool and Manchester. A land agent named William James had first thought of the idea in 1803, but it wasn't until 1822 that he had enough money to form a company and put his idea into action.

James hired George Stephenson to survey a route for the railroad. The route Stephenson chose had many challenges, including a stretch that crossed a bog. It took months for Stephenson's workers to drain the bog and establish a stable bed for the track. Critics said running a railroad across the bog was "the scheme of a madman; ignorance almost inconceivable."[4]

Other people insulted Stephenson himself. Edward Alderson, a lawyer opposed to the Liverpool and Manchester Railway, said that it was "the most absurd scheme that ever entered into the head of a man to conceive. . . . Mr. Stephenson . . . never had a plan—I believe he never had one—I do not believe he is capable of making one."[5]

However, Stephenson ignored his critics and was able to build the rail bed. He also had to build bridges over several rivers and deep valleys. The railway line would have double tracks along its route so two trains could pass each other. It would also be the first line to have passenger stations at each end of the route.

The tracks were laid 4 feet, 8.5 inches (1.4 meters) apart. This measurement became known as the English gauge. Stephenson used this measurement because it was about the same as the measurement used on the tracks in English collieries. Later the English government made it the standard gauge for all of England. It eventually became the standard gauge around the world, including in the United States, although early rail systems there sometimes used different gauges.

Once the line was mapped out, the directors of the proposed railway had to decide whether to use locomotives or stationary engines, which would sit in place along the tracks and haul the trains by cables. Some of the directors wanted to put a series of stationery engines along the tracks, but others wanted to use locomotives.

The directors decided to solve the problem with a contest. To encourage engineers to develop the best locomotive for the job, they offered a prize of £500 (then worth about $2,300—and a small fortune at the time). The candidates were tested on a completed two-mile (three-kilometer) section of level tracks in October of 1829. These tests were called the Rainhill Trials. Ten locomotives were scheduled to compete, but only five showed up for the first day of tests on October 6.

One was powered by two horses walking on a treadmill inside the carriage. It was disqualified. Another was damaged on the way to the trials. Its builder finally repaired it, but he withdrew it from the competition after it only reached a top speed of six miles (nine and a half kilometers) per hour.

That left three contenders: a locomotive built by George Stephenson and his son, Robert, called *Rocket;* Timothy Hackworth's *Sanspareil;* and an engine called *Novelty,* built by the team of John Braithwaite and John Ericsson.

Timothy Hackworth's *Sanspareil* did well early on in the Rainhill Trials, until a cracked cylinder knocked it out of the running. The locomotive was used on railways until 1844. Later it was restored and given to a British museum.

The *Rocket*

Sanspareil and *Novelty* both suffered from mechanical problems as the trials wore on. *Rocket* was the clear winner. It hauled thirteen tons at an average of twelve miles (nineteen kilometers) per hour. During one run, when it was pulling a light load of passengers, it blazed along at thirty miles (forty-eight kilometers) per hour. When the Liverpool and Manchester Railway opened in 1830, its first locomotives were built at the workshop George Stephenson had set up seven years earlier with his son and other partners, called Robert Stephenson and Company, in Newcastle.

When the Stephensons were building *Rocket,* one of the men helping them, Henry Booth, suggested that the engine use a boiler with multiple tubes. The father-and-son team agreed, and this feature was one of the main reasons the *Rocket* did so well in the trials. It had twenty-five copper tubes heating the water inside its boiler. With its multi-tubular boiler and steam-blast technology, the *Rocket* really was a rocket in its time. It would be the standard engine used in locomotives for many years.

George Stephenson died in 1848. He lived long enough to see his son, Robert, become a successful engineer. He also lived long enough to see railroads and locomotives spread all over the face of Europe. Stephenson's efforts, along with the work of Richard Trevithick, William Hedley, and the other engineers and dreamers who came before him, created the birth of the locomotive and helped change the world.

No Railroads, Please!

A train meets a tractor

Edward Alderson was not the only person who thought building railroads was a terrible idea. Many people were furious and determined to stop the railroads from being built. People who lived near where a railroad would be built did not want the tracks on their land. Many felt the noise of the trains would scare their livestock and ruin their quality of life. Farmers worried that no one would buy their oats or hay to feed horses and other livestock if railroads became popular. Their source of income would be destroyed. Canal owners feared that they would go out of business if railroads became a popular means of transportation. Teachers at Eton, one of England's finest colleges, protested the smoke and dirt the steam engines would create, and said a railway would cause students to miss classes.

Some public figures and politicians vowed that they would never travel by rail. People even made wills leaving their money to relatives only on the condition that they would never travel by rail. Railroad workers learned to conduct property surveys when the landowners were not at home so they would not be threatened or chased off the property. All of these efforts were useless, however. Nothing could stop the progress of the railroad.

1712   Thomas Newcomen invents the first commercial steam engine.

1769   Nicolas Joseph Cugnot builds a steam-powered carriage.

1784   James Watt takes out a patent for a wheeled carriage powered by a steam engine. William Murdoch builds a model of a steam-powered carriage.

1790   Nathan Read applies for a patent for a steam carriage with two cylinders. His design includes a multi-tubular boiler.

1796   Richard Trevithick starts building working models of a steam locomotive.

1801   Trevithick tests his road locomotive, *Puffing Devil,* on December 24.

1804   Trevithick demonstrates *Penydarren,* the first steam engine to run on rails.

1808   Trevithick opens an attraction in London and sells rides on the *Catch Me Who Can.*

1811   John Blenkinsop patents a rail with metal teeth. Blenkinsop's partner, Matthew Murray, develops a locomotive with two cylinders.

1812   Trevithick invents the Cornish boiler.

1813   William Hedley builds the *Puffing Billy,* and later the *Wylam Dilly.* Both work at the Wylam colliery.

1814   George Stephenson builds the *Blücher* and uses steam-blast technology.

1821   Edward Pease hires Stephenson to be chief engineer of the Stockton and Darlington Railway.

1825   The Stockton and Darlington Railway opens on September 27. Timothy Hackworth develops a more powerful engine called *Royal George.*

1829   Stephenson's engine, *Rocket,* wins the Rainhill Trials held by the Liverpool and Manchester Railway.

1830   The Liverpool and Manchester Railway opens, and uses locomotives built by Robert Stephenson and Company.

Chapter 1. A Race Between the Past and the Future

1. M. (Michael) Heavisides, *The History of the First Public Railway, (Stockton & Darlington) The Opening Day, and What Followed* (Stockton-on-Tees, England: Heavisides & Son, 1912), p. 58.
2. John Metcalfe, "Stockton & Darlington Railway: The Opening," http://www.railcentre.co.uk/stockton/opening.htm
3. Rodney Dale, *Early Railways* (Oxford, England: Oxford University Press, 1994), p. 29.
4. M. (Michael) Heavisides, *The History of the First Public Railway, (Stockton & Darlington) The Opening Day, and What Followed* (Stockton-on-Tees, England: Heavisides & Son, 1912), p. 66
5. Ibid., p. 67

Chapter 3. Captain Dick's Engines

1. Grace's Guide: British Industrial History, "Life of Richard Trevithick by F. Trevithick: Volume1: Chapter7," http:www.gracesguide.co.uk/Life_of_Richard_Trevithick_by_F._Trevithick:_Volume_1:_Chapter_7
2. Ibid.
3. M.J.T. Lewis, "Steam on the Penydarren," *The Industrial Railway Record,* No. 59, April 1975, pp. 12–32, http://www.irsociety.co.uk/Archives/59/Locos.htm
4. Ibid.
5. Sanjay Rana, *Steam Circus: A Brief History and Digital Reconstruction, 2008–2010,* http://www.steamcircus.info/index.html

Chapter 4. A Blast of Steam

1. Cotton Times: Understanding the Industrial Revolution, "John Blenkinsop and the Cogwheel Railway," http://www.cottontimes.co.uk/blenko.htm

Chapter 5. The First Railways

1. Rodney Dale, *Early Railways* (Oxford, England: Oxford University Press, 1994), p. 28.
2. John Simkin, *Spartacus Educational* biography of George Stephenson, http://www.spartacus.schoolnet.co.uk/RAstephensonG.htm
3. Stockton & Darlington Railway: "Locomotion Steams in the New Era to 21-Gun Salute and Nine Cheers," *The Northern Echo,* June 16, 2008, http://www.thenorthernecho.co.uk/history/railway/stockton/3166656.Locomotion_steams_in_the_new_era_to_21_gun_salute_and_nine_cheers/
4. Rodney Dale, *Early Railways* (Oxford, England: Oxford University Press, 1994), p. 31.
5. Samuel Smiles, *Lives of the Engineers* (London: John Murray, Albemarle Street, 1879), p. 81. From the Project Gutenberg e-book transcribed by Les Bowler.

Dale, Rodney. *Early Railways*. Oxford, England: Oxford University Press, 1994.

Houk, Randy. "Railroad History: Important Milestones in English and American Railway Development." http://www.sdrm.org/history/timeline

Lewis, M.J.T. "Steam on the Penydarren." *The Industrial Railway Record, No. 59,* April 1975, http://www.irsociety.co.uk/Archives/59/Penydarren.htm

Making the Modern World: "Constructing the Railway System." http://www.makingthemodernworld.org.uk/stories/the_age_of_the_engineer/

The Northern Echo: "Stockton & Darlington Railway: The History of the World's First Passenger Railway." http://www.thenorthernecho.co.uk/history/railway/stockton

Railroads and Trains: "William Hedley." http://railroadsandtrains.com/?p=213

Ross, David. "George Stephenson." Britain Express. http://www.britainexpress.com/History/bio/stephenson.htm

Trevithick, Francis. *Life of Richard Trevithick With an Account of His Inventions*. London: E. & F. N. Spon, 1872. From the e-book at Grace's Guide: British Industrial History.

FURTHER READING

Books

Coiley, John. *Train (DK Eyewitness Books)*. New York: Dorling Kindersley Publishing, 2009.

Curlee, Lynn. *Trains*. New York: Antheneum Books for Young Readers, 2009.

Isaacs, Sally Senzell. *The First Railroads (The American Adventure)*. Chicago: Heinemann-Raintree Classroom, 2004.

Matthews, John R. *Inventions That Shaped the World: The Railroad*. New York: Franklin Watts, 2005.

Zimmerman, Karl. *Steam Locomotives: Whistling, Chugging, Smoking Iron Horses of the Past.* New York: Boyds Mill Press, 2004.

On the Internet
Biography: George Stephenson
    http://www.helium.com/items/2147260-george-stephenson
First Trains
    http://www.familyandfriends-railcard.co.uk/cardholders/kidszone/
    railway-history/first_trains
How Does the Steam Engine Work?
    http://www.pitara.com/discover/5wh/online.asp?story=28
Rail Transport: A Timeline
    http://www.kidcyber.com.au/topics/railtran.html
All About Trains! A Children's Guide
    http://trainhornsdelivered.com/allabtrchgu.html
Steam Train Facts
    http://www.houseandhome.org/steam-train-facts

GLOSSARY

axle (AK-suhl)—A rod in the center of a wheel. On a train, each pair of wheels is connected by a straight axle, and called a wheel set.

bankruptcy—(BANK-ruhpt-see)—The state of being unable to pay back debts.

barges (BAR-juhz)—Long, flat-bottomed boats, usually used to carry freight.

canal (kuh-NAL)—A channel dug across land to connect two bodies of water.

colliery (KAHL-uh-ree)—A coal mine and the buildings and equipment associated with it.

commercial (kuh-MER-shuhl)—Something run to make money

crank—A part of an axle or shaft bent at right angles, for converting up-and-down motion to circular motion and vice versa.

crankpin—A pin by which a connecting rod is attached to a crank.

crosshead—A bar or block between the piston rod and the connecting rod in a steam engine.

driveshaft—A rotating shaft that transmits torque, or a twisting force, in an engine.

efficient (uh-FISH-uhnt)—Something that works well and doesn't waste energy.

engineer (en-juh-NEER)—A person who designs and builds engines, machines, or public works. On a train, the engineer is the driver.

exhaust (eg-ZAWST)—Waste gases produced by an engine.

flammable (FLAM-a-buhl)—Easily set on fire.

flywheel—A heavy revolving wheel in a machine that keeps spinning steadily, even when power to the machine is delivered choppily.

freight (FRAYT)—Goods carried by trains, ships, trucks, or planes.

friction (FRIK-shuhn)—A force that slows down objects when they rub against each other.

gauge (GAGE)—The distance between the rails in a railroad track.

locomotive (loh-kuh-MOH-tiv)—An engine used to pull railroad cars.

ore—A naturally occurring solid material that contains metal or minerals.

patent (PAT-uhnt)—A legal document that gives an inventor the sole rights to make or sell the invention.

stationary—(STA-shuhn-ary) Not moving; fixed in place.

traction (TRAK-shuhn)—The grasping of a body on the surface on which it moves, as of a wheel on a rail.

vacuum (VAK-yoom)—A space from which most of the air has been removed.

valve (VALV)—A part that controls the flow of liquid or gas through a pipe.

ABOUT THE
AUTHOR

Joanne Mattern is the author of more than 200 nonfiction books for young readers. Her books for Mitchell Lane include biographies of notables such as Michelle Obama, Count Basie, Benny Goodman, Blake Lively, Selena, Lebron James, and Peyton Manning. Soon after she graduated from college, Joanne took a transcontinental trip on the railroad from San Francisco to New York, an experience that opened her eyes to the huge variety of landscapes and lifestyles in the United States. Joanne especially enjoys traveling and exploring new places. She lives in New York State with her husband, four children, and an assortment of pets.